MW01491842

MEXICAN AMERICAN WAR 1846 - 1848

CAUSES, SURRENDER AND TREATIES

TIMELINES OF HISTORY FOR KIDS
6TH GRADE SOCIAL STUDIES

BABY PROFESSOR
EDUCATION KIDS

Speedy Publishing LLC
40 E. Main St. #1156
Newark, DE 19711
www.speedypublishing.com
Copyright 2018

All Rights reserved. No part of this book may be reproduced or used in any way or form or by any means whether electronic or mechanical, this means that you cannot record or photocopy any material ideas or tips that are provided in this book.

In this book, we're going to talk about the Mexican American War. So, let's get right to it!

The United States and the newly independent country of Mexico fought in the Mexican-American War from 1846 to 1848. However, the reasons that the war was started began more than twenty years before.

FLAG OF MEXICO

MEXICO BECOMES INDEPENDENT FROM SPAIN

At one time, Mexico belonged to the European country of Spain. However, the people of Mexico wanted to have their own country. Just like the citizens of the American colonies fought against their parent country, Britain, the country of Mexico did the same.

Brave Mexican generals gathered impoverished farmers to become soldiers as they fought against the Spanish. After many years of persistent fighting, the Mexican armies wore down the Spanish armies and gained their independence. They were free from Spain in the year 1821.

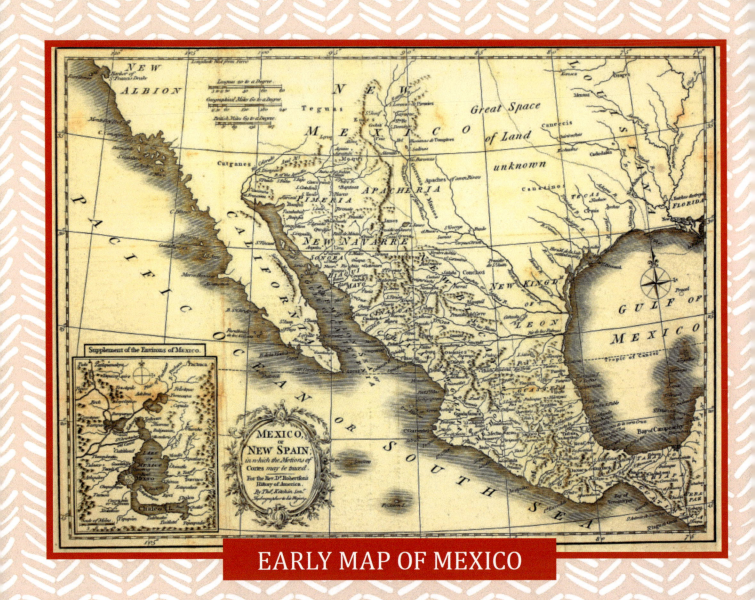

EARLY MAP OF MEXICO

THE UNITED STATES OF MEXICO

The new independent country of Mexico drafted their own constitution in the year 1824 and they called themselves the "United States of Mexico." The landmass that was part of the new country covered all of what we know today as Mexico plus what is now the western portion of the US. At that time, the land they controlled was larger than the land controlled and owned by the United States.

GENERAL SANTA ANNA GAINS POWER

However, there was unrest among the people of Mexico. Many people simply didn't want to abide by the new constitution and government. There was a fight for governmental control since several different officials claimed they had won the position of the country's president.

GOVERNMENT PALACE

ANTONIO LOPEZ DE SANTA ANNA

As often happens when there is chaos in the government, a strong leader moves forward and takes control by force. This is what happened in Mexico. A powerful general by the name of Antonio Lopez de Santa Anna overthrew the government and proclaimed himself to be President of the United States of Mexico.

Some of the citizens in the different states of Mexico didn't accept Santa Anna as their new president. To enforce his position, Santa Anna took his army and defended his government against rebel uprisings within the country.

GOVERNMENT VERSUS THE REBELS

MAP OF TEXAS STATE

TEXAS WAS A MEXICAN STATE

As the population of the United States began to grow, settlers began to spread out into surrounding territories and lands that didn't yet belong to the US. At this time, Texas was a state that belonged to Mexico, but that didn't stop US citizens from moving there and taking land to ranch and farm. These Texans didn't want to follow the government run by General Santa Anna.

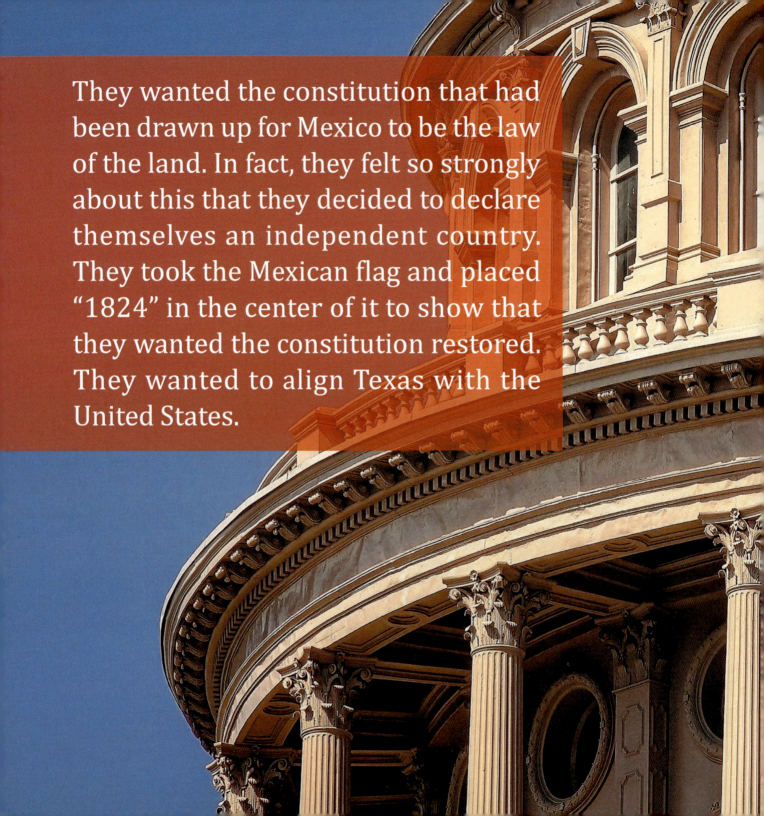

They wanted the constitution that had been drawn up for Mexico to be the law of the land. In fact, they felt so strongly about this that they decided to declare themselves an independent country. They took the Mexican flag and placed "1824" in the center of it to show that they wanted the constitution restored. They wanted to align Texas with the United States.

THE BATTLE BETWEEN TEXAS AND MEXICO

The citizens of Texas were hoping that the United States would help them in their desire to be free from General Santa Anna's government. After all, these citizens spoke the English language and were formerly from regions that were part of the United States.

They wanted Texas to have a culture more like the US. However, the US didn't get involved at first. This didn't deter the Texans from fighting Santa Anna. They gathered together their own army of Texas soldiers. Santa Anna's army was much larger and had more weapons. When the Mexican general brought his forces to Texas he was victorious first at Goliad and then at the Alamo.

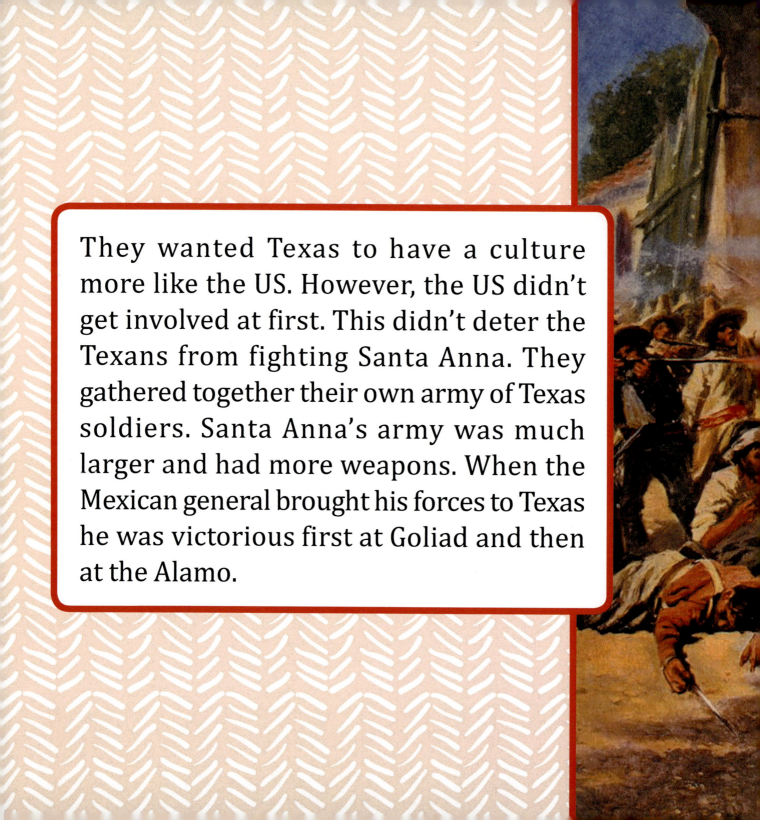

BATTLE OF THE ALAMO

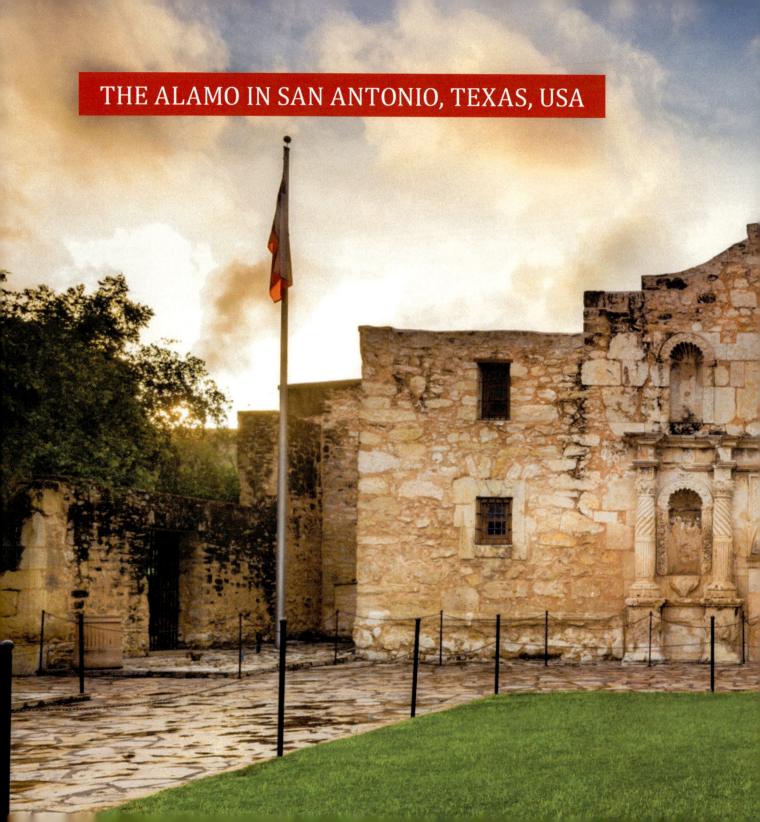

THE ALAMO IN SAN ANTONIO, TEXAS, USA

In fact, at the Alamo, Santa Anna didn't take any prisoners. Every Texan soldier was killed in that battle. This is why in Texas they have the saying "Remember the Alamo." Despite all of this, the Texans still didn't want to give up their chance for independence.

THE BATTLE OF SAN JACINTO

After the Alamo, General Santa Anna and his forces pursued the Texas armies deeper into the desert region of Texas. Texas is a very large piece of land, and after this long and arduous chase, the Mexican armies grew weary. That was when the Texas armies had their opportunity. They attacked Santa Anna's forces and were victorious at the Battle of San Jacinto.

BATTLE OF JACINTO

This decisive victory meant that Texas considered itself an independent country. They appointed Sam Houston, who had led the decisive victory at the Battle of San Jacinto, as their president. They began to write their own laws even though Santa Anna was still trying to invade and overthrow them.

THE STATUE OF SAM HOUSTON IN HERMANN PARK

TEXAS BECOMES A STATE

It took Sam Houston a decade, but he finally persuaded the US to make Texas a state. At that point in time, there were only 27 US states so Texas became the 28th. With the Mexicans still threatening Texas, it was time for the United States to step in and protect what was now their territory. What sparked the conflict was a border dispute.

MONTANA

NORTH DAKOTA

MINNESOTA

MAINE

VERMONT

NEW HAMPSHIRE

WYOMING

SOUTH DAKOTA

WISCONSIN

MICHIGAN

NEW YORK

MASSACHUSETTS

CONNECTICUT

RHODE ISLAND

UTAH

NEBRASKA

IOWA

INDIANA

OHIO

PENNSYLVANIA

NEW JERSEY

DELAWARE

MARYLAND

COLORADO

KANZAS

ILLINOIS

MISSOURI

KENTUCKY

WEST VIRGINIA

VIRGINIA

NEW MEXICO

OKLAHOMA

ARKANZAS

TENNESSEE

NORTH CAROLINA

SOUTH CAROLINA

TEXAS

LOUISIANA

MISSISSIPPI

ALABAMA

GEORGIA

FLORIDA

USA MAP WITH STATES

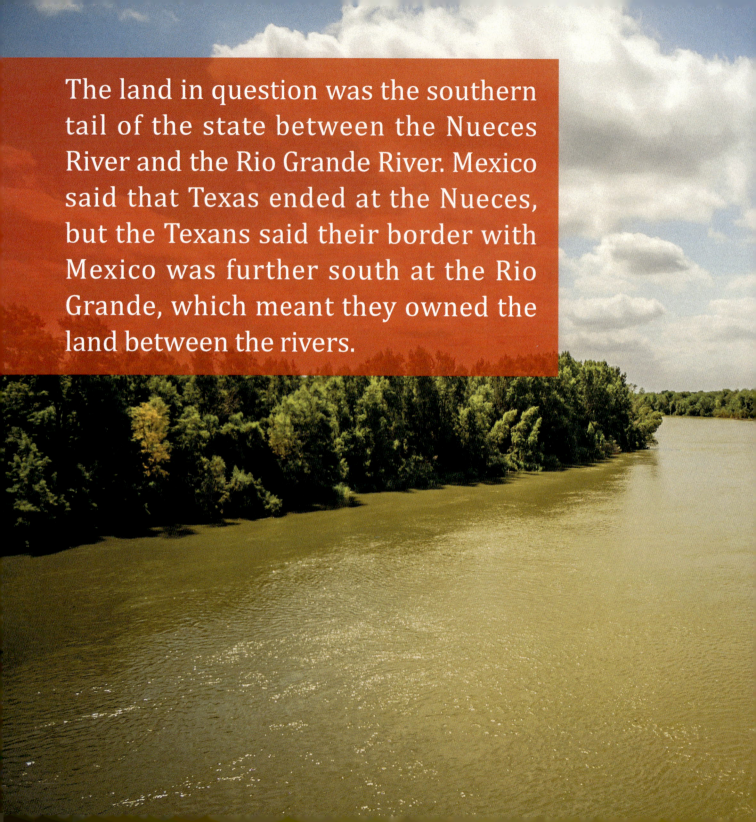

The land in question was the southern tail of the state between the Nueces River and the Rio Grande River. Mexico said that Texas ended at the Nueces, but the Texans said their border with Mexico was further south at the Rio Grande, which meant they owned the land between the rivers.

RIO GRANDE, TEXAS, USA - MEXICO BORDER

PRESIDENT JAMES K. POLK TAKES A STAND

The eleventh President of the United States, President James K. Polk, convinced the members of the US Congress to proclaim a declaration of war with Mexico in 1846. Some members of Congress didn't want to go forward. Both John Quincy Adams, who had been the sixth United States President, and Abraham Lincoln, who would later serve as the sixteenth President, didn't agree with the vote for war.

JAMES K. POLK

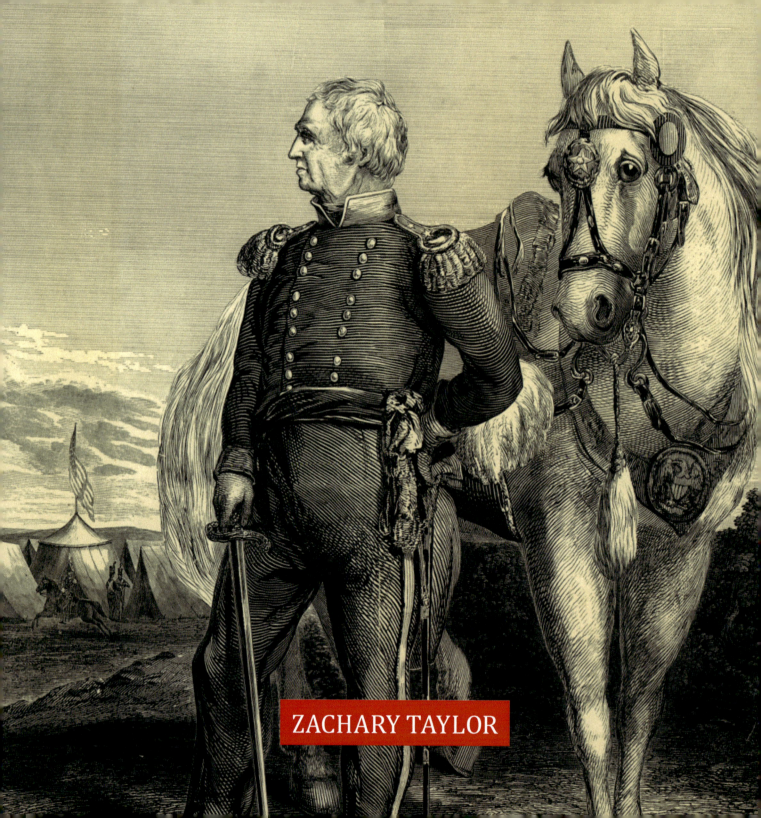

ZACHARY TAYLOR

General Zachary Taylor had constructed a fort on the land located between the Nueces and the Rio Grande. The Mexican soldiers laid siege to the fort. Taylor dispatched additional troops, but Arista, the Mexican general, and his troops stopped the reinforcements before they arrived and several major battles took place. Taylor and his troops were able to take the Mexican armies' artillery. Without weapons, the Mexican armies had to return to Mexico.

CALIFORNIA WANTS TO JOIN AMERICA TOO

Following the precedent that took place in Texas, a group of American settlers in California began to rebel against their country of Mexico as well. They proclaimed that California was now independent. Soon the US sent troops to help them become established as separate from Mexico.

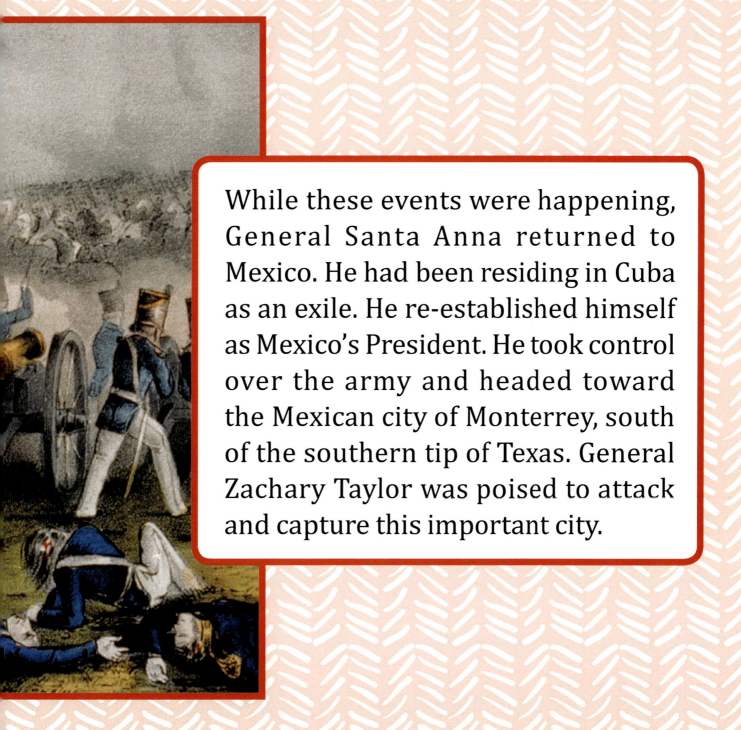

While these events were happening, General Santa Anna returned to Mexico. He had been residing in Cuba as an exile. He re-established himself as Mexico's President. He took control over the army and headed toward the Mexican city of Monterrey, south of the southern tip of Texas. General Zachary Taylor was poised to attack and capture this important city.

THE BATTLE AT MONTERREY

The Mexican people were furious that their forces had lost battles to the Americans in both Texas as well as California. When Santa Anna marched into Monterrey, he had three times the number of soldiers than Taylor. Two young American soldiers, Jefferson Davis and Braxton Bragg, were able to hold the United States line.

BATTLE AT MONTERREY

JEFFERSON DAVIS

Later in US history, Davis would become the President of the Confederate States. So many lives were lost on both sides of the conflict that neither group could continue the fight and had to obtain more soldiers and supplies.

THE CAPTURE OF MEXICO CITY

Then, President Polk made a very important military decision. Instead of dispatching reinforcements for Taylor, he sent troops under the command of General Winfield Scott via ship to the port of Vera Cruz located on the Gulf of Mexico. The Americans marched toward Mexico's capital, Mexico City. The two generals and their troops came face to face at the halfway point of Cerro Gordo.

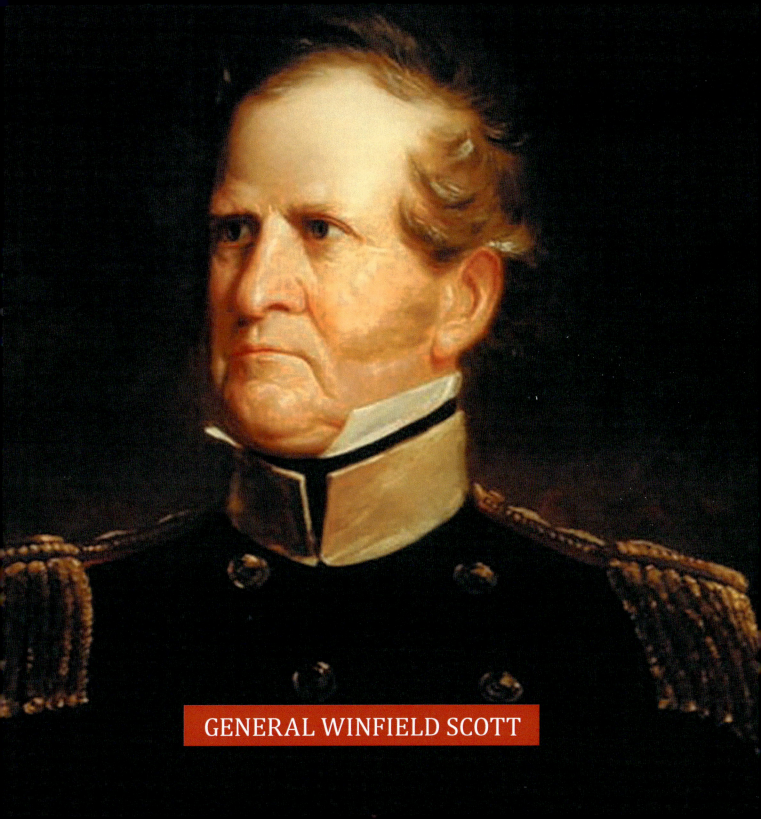

GENERAL WINFIELD SCOTT

United States troops had packed a lot of artillery and the Mexican troops charged into it. The US lost 400 soldiers, but Santa Anna lost ten times that number. Most of the Mexican soldiers were taken prisoner. The Mexicans retreated to Mexico City and the Americans pursued.

An arduous battle took place at the capital city. Two young heroes of the Mexico City battle were Robert E. Lee, who would later be a Confederate general, and Ulysses S. Grant, who would later command the opposing Union forces in the Civil War. Mexico City was captured and the United States had won the brief two-year war.

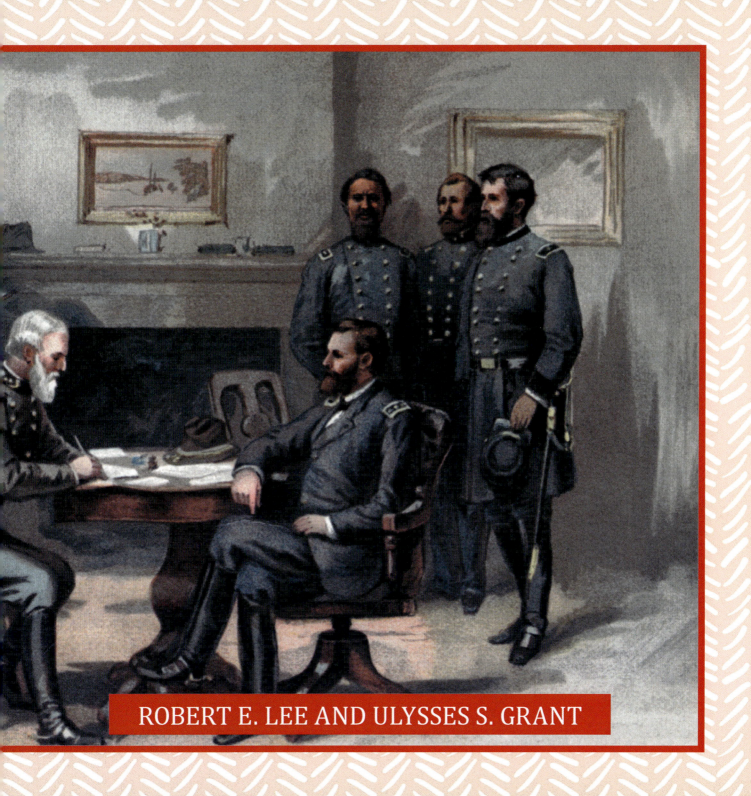

ROBERT E. LEE AND ULYSSES S. GRANT

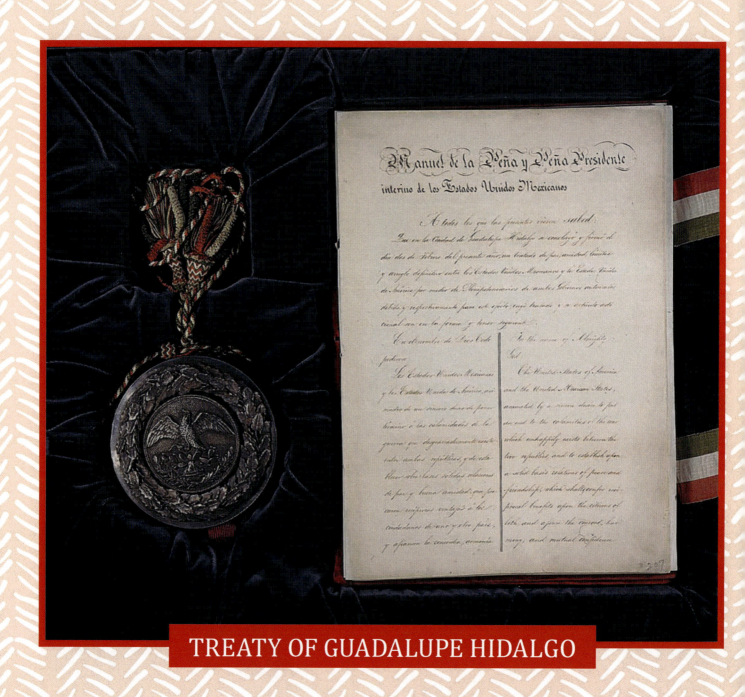

TREATY OF GUADALUPE HIDALGO

MEXICO LOSES A LARGE PORTION OF LAND

The war officially ended in February of 1848 and the Treaty of Guadalupe Hidalgo was signed. The United States took a large portion of the lands owned by Mexico, which eventually became the section of seven western states, either in whole or part. They also gave up all rights to lands in Texas. The United States paid the Mexican government $15 million. Many Mexican people are still very angry about the takeover of their lands by the Americans.

TIMELINE OF MAJOR EVENTS IN THE MEXICAN-AMERICAN WAR

May 1846—Congress makes a proclamation of war with Mexico.

July 1846—The Battle of Monterrey takes place.

March 1847—General Scott lands at Vera Cruz with his troops.

September 1847—The Battle of Mexico City takes place.

February 1848—The Treaty of Guadalupe Hidalgo is signed.

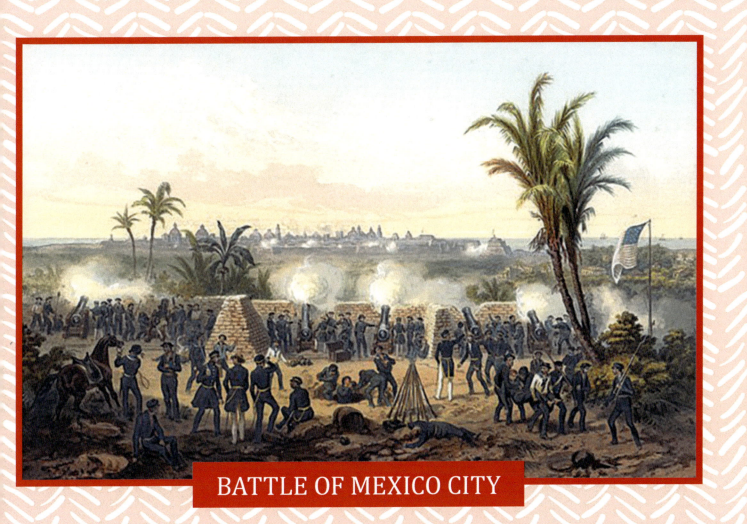

BATTLE OF MEXICO CITY

SUMMARY

After Mexico fought Spain and gained its independence, the country soon had another enemy in the form of the United States. The American population was expanding into Texas and into the west. Once Texas sought its independence from Mexico and became a state, Mexico was vulnerable to future attack. The United States expanded to the west coast once US armies were victorious against the Mexican armies in the Mexican-American War.

Awesome! Now that you've read about the history of the Mexican American War, you may want to read about politics in the United States in the 1800s in the Baby Professor book, U.S. Politics 1801-1840 - History for Children | Timelines for Kids - Historical Facts | 5th Grade Social Studies.

Visit

BABY PROFESSOR
EDUCATION KIDS

www.BabyProfessorBooks.com

to download Free Baby Professor eBooks
and view our catalog of new and exciting
Children's Books

Made in the USA
Columbia, SC
28 November 2020

25572553R00038